**PRESENTING THE**

# HISTORY IN THE LANDSCAPE

John Porter

Oxford University Press 1988

2

# Contents

# 1 Stonehenge: a famous monument

On Salisbury Plain there is a very famous **ancient monument** called Stonehenge. You have probably seen pictures of it before, or perhaps even visited it. It is now in ruins. At one time Stonehenge was made up of two circles of stone slabs, one inside the other. It was built by raising pairs of stone slabs on to their ends, and then lifting another slab called a lintel on top of them. The building of Stonehenge was started almost 5,000 years ago, at a time called the Neolithic Age or New Stone Age. It was an important centre in **prehistoric** times. In those days, people would have travelled to Stonehenge from many parts of Britain. Perhaps one reason why so many people visited Stonehenge was so that they could worship the sun, moon, and stars.

## Building Stonehenge

People have always found Stonehenge an impressive sight and have often tried to work out how it was built. Some of the stones used are far bigger than others. The smaller stones are nevertheless very big – they weigh about four tons each. They were brought from South Wales. The larger stones shown in the pictures each weigh a massive 26 tons. This is about the weight of four double-decker buses. They had to be dragged 32 km to Stonehenge from where the stone for them was found. The upright ones stand over 6 m high. Try to work out how prehistoric man, without modern machinery, managed to lift the lintel stones up on to the uprights – remember how much they weigh!

*Above:* Stonehenge as we see it now, with only a few of the huge stones left standing.

*Below:* Stonehenge from the east, as it might have appeared about 1550 BC.

**Dating Stonehenge**

Radiocarbon dating of wood fragments, ash, and pieces of bone found at Stonehenge have all helped in the dating of the monument itself.

This method measures the amount of radioactive particles (isotopes) present in any material containing carbon. All living things absorb some of these isotopes. When plants or animals die the isotopes begins to 'decay'. The amount of decay which has taken place indicates how long ago decay started, that is, when the plant or animal was last alive.

Stonehenge hasn't always looked the same. At various times people took down the stones and arranged them in a different way. The big stones were not erected until the monument had already been there about 600 years. You can think of this as meaning that if Stonehenge had first been built at the time of the Black Death (1348–49), we would only now be putting up the big stones. The drawing on the left shows what Stonehenge must have looked like soon after the final alterations to it were made, about 1550 BC.

## Fact and mystery

There has always been a lot of mystery about Stonehenge – not just about how it was built, but about what people used it for and why it was built at all. A long trackway now called the 'Avenue' leads north-eastwards, away from the monument. On midsummer day (June 21) the rising sun shines straight down the Avenue on to Stonehenge. This has led some people to think that Stonehenge might have been used for the ceremonies connected with sun worship. Other people believe that Stonehenge was a sort of giant prehistoric computer, used for doing calculations about the stars, planets, and eclipses. The meaning and purpose of early remains like Stonehenge is often interpreted in different ways.

## Prehistoric peoples

Despite all the mystery that surrounds Stonehenge, it has taught us a great deal about early times. Compared with today there were few people in prehistoric Britain, but we know that in order to build Stonehenge they must have been well organized.

The Neolithic peoples who began the building of Stonehenge used stone tools in their farming. Then came the Bronze Age people, who made tools and wares from a mixture of copper and tin. Later still, about 2,800 years ago, Iron Age man came to Britain. Some of our oldest farms and villages date back to this time. Find all these peoples, and the time when they lived, on the time chart. □

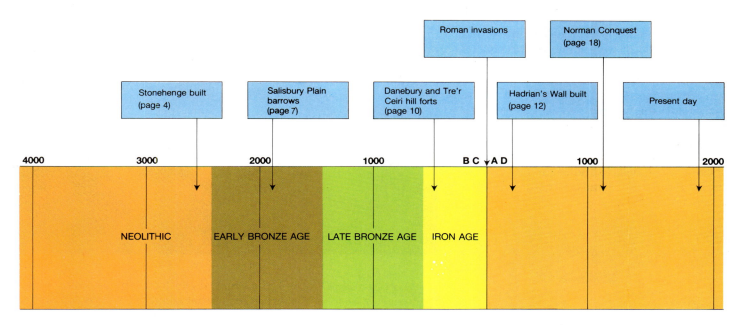

1 The small stones used for Stonehenge came from the Preseli mountains in Dyfed, South Wales. Find these on your school atlas. On tracing paper trace the coast of South Wales and the Bristol Channel. Mark on the Preseli mountains and Stonehenge. Now work out the best route for transporting four-ton blocks of stone between these two points. Remember that there were no proper roads at this time. Mark this route on you map. Add a scale. How far is it? How many different means of transport would you use? Finish your map in ink and colours. Give it a title.

2 Write down how old your father (or mother) was when you were born. Now write down the age of your father (or mother) when each of your brothers and sisters were born. Add them up and find the *average* (that is, the total of the ages divided by the number of children). Ask your friends to do the same. Compare your results with theirs—they are all probably around 30. The typical family produces a new generation about every 30 years. Look at the time chart. How many generations have there been since: a) the beginning of the Bronze Age; b) the Romans invaded Britain?

3 Some people think that early man was primitive, with no scientific or technical knowledge. From what you have read, would you agree? Give your reasons.

A time chart showing prehistoric peoples and when they lived. Most of what we think of as historical time is very recent.

The chart shows some events and monuments described in this book.

# 2 Digging up the past

Do you have snails in your garden? Most gardens have snails, but you probably don't take a lot of notice of them. There are many different sorts of snails. In prehistoric times, thousands of years even before the Romans, there were different types of snails from those we find today.

Archaeologists are people who study the past not from old writings but from surviving physical evidence – such as fragments of bone or pottery, or the ruins of buildings. They have worked out a way of using snails to show what places were like long ago. On Salisbury Plain, near Stonehenge, an archaeologist found a large mound called a **barrow**. It measured about 2 m high and 40 m long. He knew that mounds like this were built by prehistoric people. He dug down through the barrow and then beneath it. This is called **excavation**. From the various sorts of snail shells he found underneath the barrow, he worked out that before the barrow was built the land had been covered in grass. Many centuries before that, it had been forest. Of course he needed to know a lot about snail shells to find all this out. Look at the diagram below to find out more about how he went about it.

A long barrow similar to the one from which the soil profile was taken.

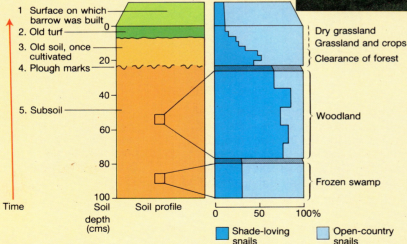

An archaeologist recorded the types of snails that he found at different depths in the soil under a barrow. Some snails were shade-loving types that lived under trees. Others were open-country snails that preferred grassland. He drew the diagram shown above right. Lots of open-country snails meant that the vegetation had probably been grassland when they lived in the soil. Remember that the deeper you dig, the older the soil is.

The snail shells told him an interesting story. It seems that about 10,000 years ago the ground had been frozen swamp. Then, as the centuries passed, the weather got warmer and forest began to grow. About 6,000 years ago some farmers came along, looking for somewhere to live. They felled the forest and used the land for grazing or pasture. This was so that they could graze their herds of cattle and sheep. They farmed the land like this for many generations. About 4,800 years ago their descendants needed to bury an important member of their community who had just died. They made a tomb for his body with stone slabs and covered it with a huge mound of earth. The barrow they had made remained undisturbed until our archaeologist decided to dig it up just a few years ago.

Without the help of the snail shells, the part of the story before the building of the barrow could not have been worked out.

6

## Round barrows and long barrows

On Salisbury Plain there are many other barrows besides the one you have just read about. Long ago, people felt that they should mark the places where important people were buried. They made their barrows in various shapes – some were long, others were round. The diagram shows the different types. Many of the ones on Salisbury Plain are *round* barrows. Most of them date from a time called the 'Bronze Age'. Nearly 300 years ago, another archaeologist called William Stukeley stood on Salisbury Plain and made a drawing of all the barrows he could see. Look at his drawing. There are very many barrows. You would find far fewer now. This is because today's big farming machines have levelled out most of them. Many people think we should now try to keep the ones that are left, so that future generations will be able to see what barrows were like.

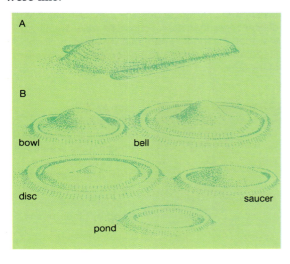

*Above:* Lambourn Seven Barrows, a group of round barrows in Berkshire. This is an *oblique* aerial photograph, that is, one that is taken at an angle to the ground.

*Left:* Types of barrows: A is a *long* barrow, B shows different types of *round* barrow.

*Below:* William Stukeley's sketch of barrows near Stonehenge. He drew this in 1723.

## What archaeologists do

Archaeologists have many ways of finding the history in the landscape. The study of snails is only one of them. They make drawings and plans of old banks and ditches. These are called **earthworks**, and sometimes mark the sites of old buildings, defences, or boundaries. Archaeologists often find ancient sites by studying **aerial photographs**. These are pictures of the ground taken from a low-flying aeroplane. The archaeologists excavate the most important sites and record the results. Sometimes they can also learn something about the history of a site from its soil. Our archaeologist above used the snail remains in the soil.

In the next few pages you can learn more about these and other methods used by archaeologists. □

1  Frozen swamp is called **tundra**. Do you know of any other parts of the world which still have tundra conditions?

2  Count up the number of barrows in William Stukeley's picture. Why are many of them no longer there? Why is it important to preserve the ones that are left?

3  Study the photograph of Lambourn Seven Barrows. Name the different types of barrows shown in the picture.

4  What is 'archaeology'? How do archaeologists help us to understand the past? What techniques do they use to do this?

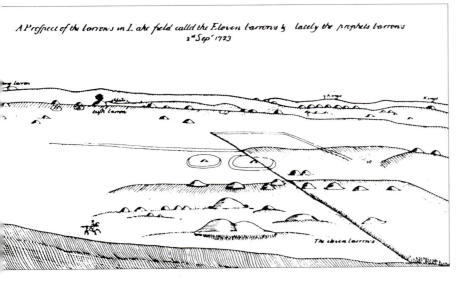

# 3 A fossil landscape

You may have seen fossils in your local museum. A fossil is the remains of an animal, fish, or plant which died many thousands of years ago. Its shape is preserved in sedimentary rock. Some fossils are easy to see. With others you have to study the rock very carefully indeed. Studying a fossilized rock is like seeing the past in front of your eyes. You are almost taking a journey back into time. Sometimes landscapes are like fossilized rocks. They still contain the shapes of things from the past, but you have to look hard to see them.

## Living off the land

The fossil landscape described below is not far from the River Test. It is one of many Iron Age farms discovered in this area from aerial photographs. Their positions are shown on the map. All these farms were on gently sloping land above the river valley, close to good meadow along the river for growing hay. On the drier ground the farmers could grow other crops. On high ground above the farm were the chalk hills or downs where sheep could graze. The

### A fossil landscape

The aerial photograph below shows part of Hampshire. Notice all the strange, blurred lines on the picture. These lines appear to be chaotic and disorderly. But look a bit harder. Can you pick out any shapes?

An archaeologist studied the picture and used it to draw the sketch. He knew that many of the lines were made by today's big farming machines, but he thought that others were much older. He was able to pick out the boundaries of what he thought were Iron Age fields. He also found the shape of a bank or wall which enclosed a farm site of the same age. Find these on the sketch, and notice that they all follow different lines from the modern field walls. We could say that the photograph had revealed a 'fossil' landscape. This is because it still contains the shapes of the features of past landscapes.

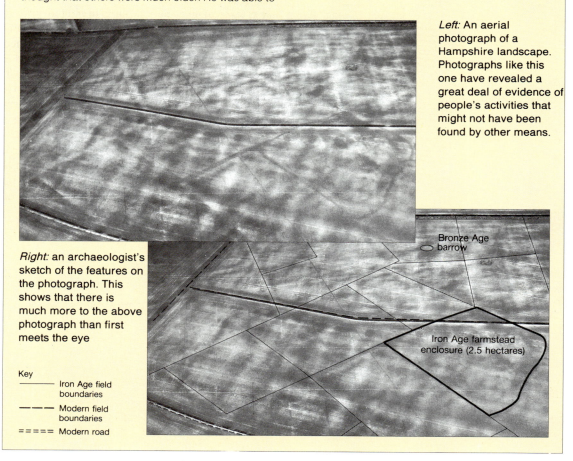

*Left:* An aerial photograph of a Hampshire landscape. Photographs like this one have revealed a great deal of evidence of people's activities that might not have been found by other means.

Bronze Age barrow

Iron Age farmstead enclosure (2.5 hectares)

*Right:* an archaeologist's sketch of the features on the photograph. This shows that there is much more to the above photograph than first meets the eye

Key

——— Iron Age field boundaries

– – – Modern field boundaries

===== Modern road

map shows that some farms were quite close together, and others were further apart. Perhaps the farms on their own were big with lots of land. Can you think of another explanation for the 'gaps' in the spacing? Remember that the map shows only the farm sites that have been *found*!

The plan inset below shows how one of these farms could have been laid out. The family had to provide everything it needed for survival from what there was around the farmstead. This is called 'self-sufficiency'. Besides growing crops and keeping livestock, the family made pots, spun and wove wool, and smelted iron for tools and weapons. The photograph shows what the farmhouse looked like. It was just one room, with walls of timber and mud. People cooked, ate, and slept around

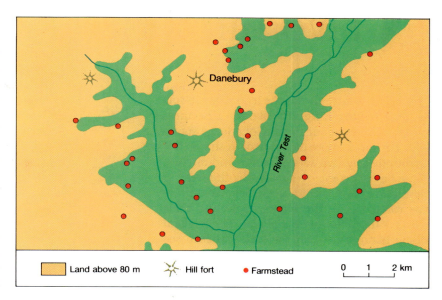

Land above 80 m     ✳ Hill fort     ● Farmstead     0    1    2 km

*Left:* Reconstruction of an Iron Age farm at Butser Hill, Petersfield.

*Above:* Iron Age farmsteads near Danesbury hill-fort.

an open hearth in the middle of the floor.

The farmers along the River Test were probably all part of a large tribal group. They had to serve a chief who would have lived at one of the bigger farms in the area. The entire community would have been administered from the **hill-fort** of Danebury (see page 10). Find this on the map. Why do you think it was a good place to have a hill-fort? What suggests to you that there was another tribal group in this area? ☐

1   Make a large copy of the map on the left. It shows an area where three Iron Age farmers are thinking of building new farms. Show the best sites for the three farmsteads on your map. To do this you have to think about what each farmer needed:
    several sorts of land near by;
    a water supply;
    lands within easy reach;
    a dry site, not marshy;
    to avoid quarrels with neighbours.
Draw in where you think the boundaries between the three farms might have been.

2   Convince a friend that in the Iron Age the countryside was well settled and organized. Use these ideas for your argument:
    farmhouses;
    field boundaries;
    hill forts;
    tribal groups.

3   How self-sufficient is your family? What skills would you need to learn for self-sufficiency?

*Above (inset)* A typical farm layout:
1-ditch and bank,
2-area for smelting iron,
3-haystacks,
4-cattle shelter,
5-rubbish pits,
6-house.
*Right:* Base map for question 1. Make an enlarged copy.

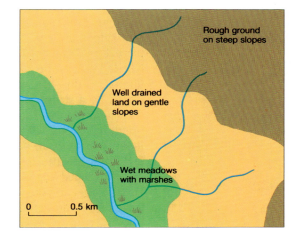

Rough ground on steep slopes

Well drained land on gentle slopes

Wet meadows with marshes

0     0.5 km

# 4 Two hill-forts

The first picture shows the Iron Age hill-fort at Danebury Ring. It is about 11 hectares in area. This is about the size of a large sports field. The fort is more or less oval in shape. It is surrounded by two sets of banks and ditches. These have become overgrown by the trees in the picture, but within these defences, there was room for all the local people and their livestock to shelter in time of war. The fort had a long history. Look at the facts panel to see when was it first built and when it was last used.

## Horns and claws

How would you have attacked this fort? The builders thought about this carefully. They worked out that the easiest point to attack was the east gate. Here they built a complicated system of ditches and **ramparts** (banks) which look like 'horns' or 'claws'. Picture what attackers would have to do. First they had to get through the hail of spears and stones thrown at them from defenders on the outer hornwork (marked A on the diagram). The next step was to batter down the outer gate. Then they faced the defenders on the 'horn' which guarded the entrance passage (marked B). The defence could be well organized from the 'command post' rampart (marked C). This was very difficult to attack successfully. Many of the attackers would probably have been killed trying to take it.

**Danebury Ring**

**Where it is**: Nether Wallop near Andover, Hampshire
**Height above sea level**: 142 m (469 ft)
**Area**: 5.3 ha (inside), 11 ha (outside)
**When built**: 5th century BC
**Last used**: time of Roman conquest

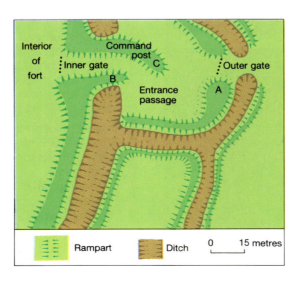

The eastern entrance of Danebury Ring hill-fort. A series of banks (ramparts) and ditches form 'horns' or 'claws' which protected the gates from attackers.

Interior of fort — Inner gate — Command post C — Outer gate — B — Entrance passage — A

Rampart    Ditch    0    15 metres

## A lunar landscape in Wales

You can find remains of hill-forts on hilltops and ridges all over Britain. Look next at the picture of Tre'r Ceiri, a hill-fort in Gwynedd, North Wales. The name means 'town of the giants'. Unlike Danebury this hill-fort is enclosed by a strong stone wall. This is because there was plenty of stone but not much soil for building. Notice all the rings inside it. They look like craters on the surface of the moon. In fact they are the foundations of huts which once crowded together inside the enclosure. How many can you count? Archeologists have found 150 altogether. Although not all the huts may have been houses, these finds show

**Tre'r Ceiri**

**Where it is**: Llanaelhaearn near Pwllehli, Gwynedd
**Height above sea level**: 482 m (1591 ft)
**Area**: 2.1 ha (inside)
**When built**: 5th century BC
**Last used**: about 300AD

that many families could have lived inside the hill-fort at any one time. Perhaps Tre'r Ceiri was used in a rather different way from Danebury. On the nearby lowland plain are the sites of over 80 old hamlets (small clusters of cottages or farms). Until recent times local people lived by keeping cattle and sheep. In the Iron Age the farmers used to drive their livestock on to the higher ground around Tre'r Ceiri for the summer. They would spend some time living in the huts inside the hill-fort. This was so that the lower land around the farms could be used for crops and hay. Like Danebury, the fort could also be used for shelter in time of war.

A few of the old farms on the lowland are still lived in. The houses themselves may have been rebuilt several times down the centuries. It is a fascinating thought that over 2,500 years ago the people who lived in these farms used to find refuge within the walls of Tre'r Ceiri. □

1 Make two headings, one for Danebury Ring, the other for Tre'r Ceiri. Make a list of facts about each fort. Are they very similar to or very different from each other?

2 'The farms and hamlets around Tre'r Ceiri were built on the better soil.' Is this true? (Look at the second diagram) Write a paragraph to explain your answer.

3 Make a large drawing of the Danebury 'horns' defences. You have 100 men with which to defend it. Decide the best places to position them and show this on the diagram. Now give the diagram to a friend. Ask him or her to work out the best way of attacking your fort.

4 Why were hill-forts important to Iron Age people?

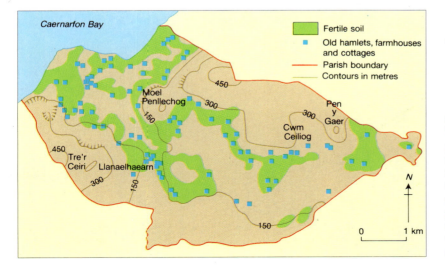

Old farm sites around Tre'r Ceiri. The hill-fort probably provided refuge for people from the surrounding lowland farms in times of danger. The main permanent settlement in the area may have been where present-day Llanaelhaearn is sited.

# 5 On the frontier

*Above:* A typical milecastle. There were double gates at front and rear.

Life was normally quiet at the small milecastle on Hadrian's wall. Occasionally the soldiers on duty opened the milecastle gate to allow a local farmer and his sheep to go through. Otherwise they didn't seem to have all that much to do.

The milecastle was one of a chain of small forts built along Hadrian's Wall. They were so called because they were about a mile apart. Hadrian's Wall was the northern frontier of Roman Britain. Look at the 'facts' on Hadrian's Wall and the map. Where is the wall? Who built it? When was it built?

Guarding the milecastle must have seemed a dull job to the half dozen or so soldiers on duty. It measured only about 60 ft each way. The only buildings in it were the small barrack block and watch tower over the gate. If you visit the ruin today you are more likely to notice the spectacular scenery around you. The wall here was built along the top of high, rocky, crags. From the wall top there are breath-taking views over open moorlands. The soldiers probably remembered the scenery only as harsh and bleak.

## Housesteads: a frontier fort

At the end of their spell of duty at the milecastle the soldiers returned to Housesteads. This was a 'frontier fort' just a quarter of mile down the wall. The Roman name was 'Vercovicium'. The frontier forts were the main garrisons along the wall. They supplied the troops who guarded the milecastles. The soldiers themselves were not regular Roman troops. They were part of a regiment recruited from the local people of Roman Britain. They were called 'auxiliaries'. Housesteads, like the other main forts on the wall, was a self-contained garrison. This means that it tried to provide for all its needs itself. The soldiers had to be able to turn their hands to several jobs. Within the walls there were barracks, stables, granaries for storing grain, workshops for repairing weapons and equipment, a hospital, headquarters building, and house for the commandant. Some of these buildings have been excavated. Look for them on the aerial photograph.

Soldiers going out of the fort on leave would have passed first through a village just outside the main gates. On the picture you can see the foundations of the excavated houses. Here, retired old soldiers and their families lived. Archaeologists have found pieces of old ironware, and the remains of cobblers' shops. The garrison would have needed these trades as well as others – such as glassmaking and pottery. It must have been a busy, bustling place in Roman times. Beyond the fort there were strips of cultivated land called 'terraces'. These show that the settlement grew some of its own food. Although few crops can grow there at the present day, archaeologists think that the climate was rather warmer and drier than it is now.

*Below:* Hadrian's Wall near Housesteads. The wall builders used the crags of the Great Whin Sill to form part of the wall.

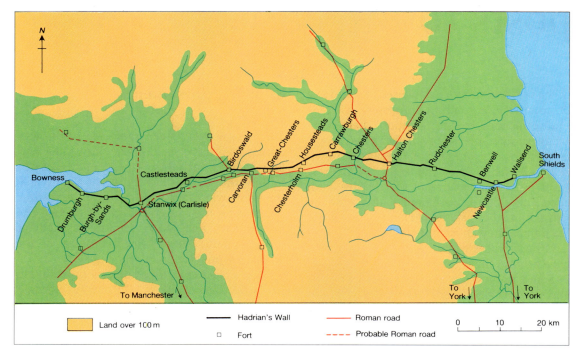

Map legend: Land over 100 m | Hadrian's Wall | Roman road | Probable Roman road | □ Fort | 0 10 20 km

## What was the wall for?

The soldiers at Housesteads might well have asked themselves what the wall was for. They would have been told that it was there to defend Roman Britain from the barbarians to the north. But they also knew that if a big attack came, the wall was too long to be properly defended. Perhaps they concluded that it was really there to stop the barbarians from coming into Roman Britain to settle. If too many of them came to live permanently among the Romanized Britons this would threaten the Roman way of life.

There have been other famous walls in history built for the same sort of purpose. About 2,000 years ago the Great Wall of China was built. This was intended to keep invaders out of northern China. It is 4,000 km long and used to have a road on top. Another famous wall is in Berlin in Germany. This wall was built in 1961 to divide Berlin into two cities. It is heavily guarded and people need permits to pass from one part of the city to the other. □

1 Look at the map showing the wall and the Roman roads. In what ways were the roads important to the troops serving on the wall?

2 Imagine you are a soldier guarding the wall. Your family lives in a Roman town in the south of Britain. Write a letter home describing your living conditions, what the frontier is like, and what you feel about it.

3 Using the map above, copy and complete the 'strip diagram' of the wall that has been started on the right. Starting with Wallsend, show on your diagram:
   a) the distances in kilometres between the forts (you will have to work these out using the scale on the map)
   b) if any roads lead from the forts, where they go.

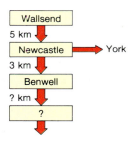

# 6 Signposts to the past

The signpost shown below used to stand at a country crossroads in Shropshire. There is a more modern looking signpost there now, but the same names are on it. Long ago people had to think of names for all the places shown on the signpost. They named some of these places from the features of the nearby landscape. Other places were named after a person with whom the place was closely connected. The names they chose now tell us a lot about how these places began, and what the landscape around them used to be like.

Some names are easier to explain than others. Ironbridge means what it says. You can still find the historic iron bridge after which the village was named. For the other places on the signpost, you would need the help of an expert to work out what the names mean. Even where the expert has explained the name for us, we may still want to ask a lot of questions about it. For instance, who was Eata? Where was the 'white monastery'?

*Below:* This kind of signpost is not seen very much nowadays. The names on it have also changed, but over a much longer period of time. These names tell us a great deal about the surrounding area.

## Using the oldest names

Place-name experts are interested in the way names *used* to be spelt, particularly their earliest known spellings. The elements in the name – that is, the different words from which the name was made up – are most interesting. Atcham on the signpost comes from two elements: 'Eata' and 'ham'. A 'ham' was a village or settlement; 'Eata' was the name of the village's founder.

Some places had many different spellings in medieval times. Look at all the ways Shrewsbury could be spelt. Shrewsbury is in Shropshire, which many people call Salop for short. You can see how this word comes from one of the old ways of writing Shrewsbury. In the name Shrewsbury, a 'bury' was a fortified place. The 'Shrew' part seems to come from 'The Scrobs' – but nobody is really sure what this means, or where it was.

| Past spellings of Shrewsbury | |
| --- | --- |
| *Date* | *Spelling* |
| 1016 | Scrobbesbyrig |
| 1100 – 1400 | Shrobesbury |
| | Shrofbury |
| | Shrouesbury |
| | Salopesberie |
| | Schrowesbury |
| 1400 – 1500 | Shrouesbury |
| | Shrowsbury |

## The Anglo-Saxons

A lot of names were first given to places by the Anglo-Saxons or early English. They began to settle in Britain about 450AD, after the Romans had left. They moved into areas where the Romanized Britons or Celts already lived. They gave the Romano-British farms and villages new names. Most of these names are still used, although the spelling may have changed quite a lot. Other places still have the old British or Celtic names today, but these are mostly in areas such as Cornwall or Wales, where the Anglo-Saxons did not settle. A few Roman names are still found, like 'Wroxeter'. Some places were named by the Vikings, who came to Britain after the Anglo-Saxons. Look at the table (p. 15, top right) of some of the main elements we can still find in today's place-names.

CRESSAGE 'Oak tree of christ'

EATON 'Farm by a river'
CONSTANTINE A family name

UPPINGTON 'The upper farm'

HARLEY 'Hare clearing'

WELLINGTON 'Enclosure made by people from the temple wood'

MUCH WENLOCK 'Large place of the white monastery'

EATON CONSTANTINE CROSS ROADS

CRESSAGE 1½
HARLEY 3
MUCH WENLOCK 5½

EATON CONSTANTINE ½
UPPINGTON 3¼
WELLINGTON 6¼

LEIGHTON 1
BUILDWAS 2¾
IRONBRIDGE 5

WROXETER 2¾
ATCHAM 4½
SHREWSBURY 8½

BUILDWAS 'Building in a wet or marshy place'

WROXETER 'A Roman town called Viriconium'

LEIGHTON Farm where leeks were grown

ATCHAM 'The village of Eata's people'

SHREWSBURY 'A fortified place at the Scrobs'

## Offa's Dyke

The earthwork shown in the picture below is called Offa's Dyke. Offa was the ruler of an old English kingdom called Mercia. He built the dyke in about 780AD to mark the western boundary of his kingdom. West of the line he chose for the dyke, the land remained in the hands of the Celtic people who became the Welsh. The present-day boundary between England and Wales still keeps close to Offa's dyke for much of its length.

Offa's Dyke also marks the limit of English place-names along the Welsh border. West of the dyke there are very few English names but a lot of Celtic or Welsh ones. Similarly there are hardly any Celtic names east of the dyke, in what was the kingdom of Mercia. The dyke was a boundary between two peoples and two languages. The two peoples are now one, but the place-names remind us of a time when life was very different. □

### Some elements often found in place-names

| Element | Meaning | Example* |
|---|---|---|
| *(British Celtic/Welsh)* | | |
| afon | stream, river | River Avon |
| tre | homestead, village | *Pentre* |
| llan | church | *Llanhedrick* |
| pen | hilltop | *Penyllan* |
| *English (Anglo-Saxon)* | | |
| ing | territory | Worthing |
| ham | homestead | *Atcham* |
| tun | village | *Bicton* |
| stoke | 'daughter' village | Basingstoke |
| stow | holy place | Chepstow |
| bury | fortified place | *Chirbury* |
| *Viking (Danish and Norse)* | | |
| by | homestead | Kirkby |
| thwaite | clearing | *Rosthwaite* |
| saetr | summer hill farm | *Seatoller* |

*The names in italics are mentioned in this book

**Offa's Dyke – a boundary between two peoples**

**West**
*Many Welsh place-names, for example:*
Pentre
Peryllan
Bacheldre
Bachaeblan
Bryn mawr
*Not many English place-names, for example:*
Hopton

**East**
*Many English place-names, for example:*
Winsbury
Chirbury
Dudston
Church Stoke
Melington
Bicton
*Not many Welsh place-names, for example:*
Cefn Eionion
Llanhedrick

1  a) Make a list of *ten* street or road names around where you live.
   b) Divide and rewrite the list in a table with *three* headings: roads named after *places*; roads named after *people*; other road names.
   c) Now rewrite the list again in another table with *two* headings: roads named after *local* people, places, features, or events; other road names.
   d) Write a paragraph called: 'How my local roads and streets have been named'.

2  From the signpost and the text, write about:
   a) a name that you can easily see the meaning of;
   b) a name that describes what the area around that place was like;
   c) a name that tells you the Romans settled not far away;
   d) a name showing that the place had religious importance;
   e) a name of a local family;
   f) a name you would like to know more about.

3  Write a paragraph explaining why the interpretations of place-names isn't always as easy as it looks.

4  Write an essay comparing Offa's Dyke and Hadrian's Wall (pages 10–11). Say whether the purpose of the dyke was very similar to, or very different from, that of the wall.

*Above:* View of Offa's Dyke taken between Montgomery and Clun. The dyke has been described as follows: 'Offa's great dyke along the Welsh border was not just a frontier. It was a base for further raids in Wales and a barrier against counter-attacks. Both Offa and his successors waged war well beyond it'.

# A Viking valley

Look at the picture of the Viking ship. Ships like this could easily float in water only a few feet deep. The Vikings used them for sailing up into rivers around the English coast. In ships like these they could easily reach places quite a long way inland.

About the year 900, groups of Vikings from Norway (Norsemen) crossed the North Sea in their long ships. They sailed up the river estuaries around the Lake District. From here they journeyed into the heart of the Lakeland mountains looking for somewhere to settle. In the narrow valleys they built farms and cleared forests for crops and grazing. Until the Norsemen came, very few people had lived in this area at all.

## A Lakeland walk

A walk along a valley and over the Lakeland mountains tells us a lot about the landscape the Norsemen found. The large map shows a valley called Borrowdale. Find on it the hamlet of Seathwaite. Now look up the name 'thwaite' on page 15. You will see that it is a Norse name. Seathwaite means 'clearing amongst the marsh grasses'. If we walk down the valley we pass other places with 'thwaite' in their names – Thorneythwaite, Burthwaite, Longthwaite, and Rosthwaite. They all mean that a long time ago the Norsemen settled in Borrowdale and they cleared wooded or marshy areas for farmland.

Another place on the way to Rosthwaite is Seatoller. This name comes from another Norse word, 'saetr'. A saetr was a hill farm. It was used for pasturing sheep on mountain grasslands in summer. The farmers using this farmstead lived further down Borrowdale. They drove their cattle and sheep up the valley just for the summer grazing. Where else in this book have farmers done the same thing? Look it up to find out why they did it (page 11).

From Rosthwaite a path climbs high on to the fellside or mountainside. From the boulders and woods of the fell there are striking views across Borrowdale. The pathway follows an old track called the 'Bowdergate'. This name means 'road by a hill farm'. It dates back to the time of the Norse farmers. They drove their cattle and sheep along it from the valley farms to the upland pastures.

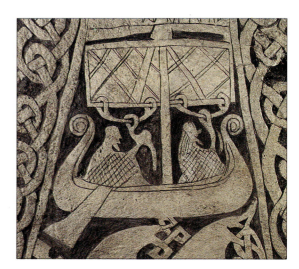

*Right:* A carving of a viking longship.

*Below:* The Borrowdale Valley in the Lake District. Many of the place names date back to the Norse invasion of about 900 AD.

*Inset below:* Areas of England and Wales where the Norsemen settled.

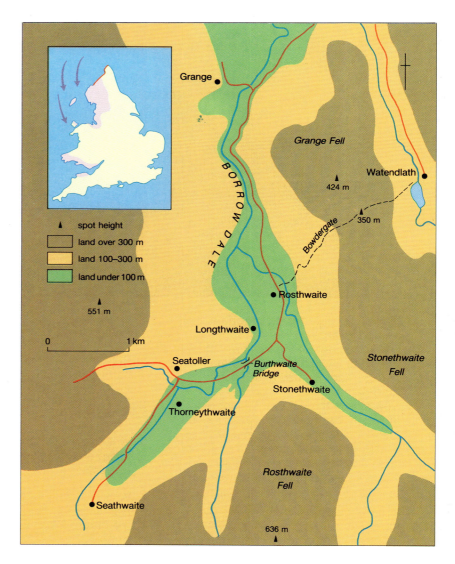

▲ spot height

▢ land over 300 m

▢ land 100–300 m

▢ land under 100 m

## A landscape of hamlets

The Bowdergate takes you into a neighbouring valley, to a hamlet called Watendlath. In the Lake District there are not many villages but a lot of hamlets like Watendlath and Rosthwaite. The Norsemen preferred to live in groups of just two or three families. Each farmer had his own pieces of grazing land. His farm often included many hundreds of acres of rough pasture on the fells. They did not share land in common fields like the Anglo-Saxons.

About 300 years after the Norsemen, most of Borrowdale was bought by the monks of Furness Abbey. This was near Barrow-in-Furness, about 30 miles away. One of the ways in which the monks lived was by keeping sheep and selling the wool. They turned a lot of Borrowdale into sheep 'ranches'. A monastic sheep farm was called a 'grange'. The word has been used for the name of a hamlet in Borrowdale. Find it on the map. In which area on the map do you think the sheep from Grange were pastured?

The Norsemen started a long tradition of sheep grazing in Borrowdale. The medieval monks continued it. The Borrowdale farmer of today drives his sheep on to the same hills used by the Norsemen of 1,000 years ago. □

*Below:* A deep inlet or fjord in Norway. The Norsemen learned to sail their long ships in areas like this. From here they sailed to found new settlements in Britain. They looked for areas similar to their homeland

*Above:* Scattered settlements in a valley in the Lake District.

1  How long do you think it would have taken a Norse farmer to walk from Rosthwaite to Watendlath? Remember the sort of countryside it is.

2  Show how place-names help us to understand how the Lakeland landscape changed over the centuries.

3  From the small inset map and your atlases, name three other counties in Britain where you might expect to find Norse place-names. List the names under the headings of the areas where they occur.

4  Write about ways in which the Norse way of life was different from that of the Anglo-Saxons. To do this ask yourself: what sorts of settlement did the Norsemen live in?; did they share land with other farmers?; what was their farming like?

5  Look at the photograph on the left. It shows a deep inlet along the coast of Norway. It is called a fjord. The Norsemen came from areas like this. Why do you think they found the Lake District so attractive?

# 8 The Domesday landscape

One day in the spring of 1086 Hugh of Powerstock received some unusual visitors. Two men arrived with a letter from the king that instructed them to carry out a survey of all the land and wealth of Hugh's village. The information was for a general survey King William the Conqueror was making of all the wealth in his kingdom. The commissioners told Hugh that he would be severely punished for concealing information or giving false facts.

Powerstock is in Dorset. Before the Norman Conquest of England in 1066, it had belonged to a Saxon nobleman called Ailmar. Now Hugh was the lord of Powerstock. He had once been a knight in the service of a Norman baron called Roger of Arundel. When Roger was granted lands in Dorset for helping him in the Conquest, he gave the village of Powerstock to Hugh for his service in battle. All this was recorded by the commissioners.

Powerstock, Dorset.

## Recording the landscape

The commissioners wanted to know how much land there was and what it was worth. They also asked about how much tax or 'geld' Hugh had previously paid for it. These facts were eventually written up (see above right) in the great book we know as *Domesday Book*. In *Domesday Book* you can find the same sort of information for most other English villages besides Powerstock.

The entry in *Domesday Book* for Powerstock is shown on this page. It is in Latin, the language in which most people wrote at the time. Notice how the value of Hugh's village had increased in the 20 years since the Conquest. This would be important when the king was deciding how much tax it should pay in the future .

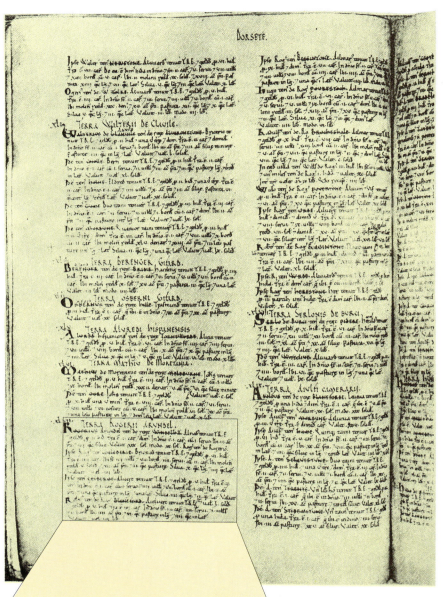

This entry in *Domesday Book* records that there was enough land in Powerstock to keep six plough teams busy. Some of it was in the lord's demesne, but the rest was farmed by peasants called 'villeins' or 'bordars'. There were also meadows, woods, pastures, and two mills.

Before the Conquest the estate was worth £4, but it had increased in value to £6.

## Using Domesday Book

Unfortunately, *Domesday Book* does not provide information about the whole country. It provides very little information about the north of England and none at all about Wales. For southern counties like Dorset, however, it is very detailed.

Historians have used the information in *Domesday Book* in a variety of ways. The pie diagram opposite is one way of representing the facts. This diagram uses the information to show how the land in Dorset was shared out. You will notice that most of the land belonged to the church, especially to the abbeys, and to Norman barons like Roger of Arundel. Some land still remained in the hands of Anglo-Saxon noblemen or 'thegns'. Some of these would have been men who decided against supporting King Harold at the Battle of Hastings.

There are other ways of showing Domesday details. The graph is a 'scattergraph' on which each dot is a village not far from Bath, in Avon. Each village is plotted according to its population and the number of plough teams it had. What conclusion can you draw from the graph? Did bigger villages always have more plough teams than smaller ones?

Maps can be drawn from *Domesday Book*. The map opposite is based on the number of plough teams for each part of the country. Fertile land will provide work for a lot of plough teams, so many plough teams means high fertility. Was your part of the country covered by the Domesday survey? Was it fertile in 1086? Perhaps your teacher will be able to answer this by showing you your local Domesday entry. □

1   What was Powerstock like in 1086? Write a few sentences describing the features of its landscape.

2   Suppose that you were organizing a present-day Domesday survey for your local area (some schools have recently been doing this for a BBC television project). Make a list of the sorts of information you would include.

3   Head two columns as shown below:

| A Fertile areas in 1086 | B Infertile areas in 1086 |
|---|---|
|  |  |

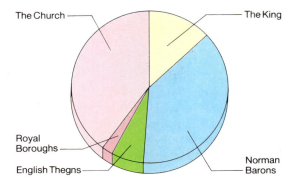

*Left:* Who owned the land of Dorset in 1086.

*Below:* A scattergraph of population (number of homes) and plough teams for a district of Avon.

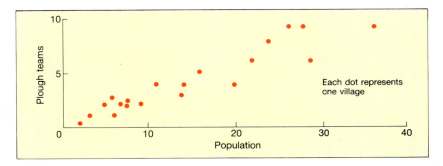

Each dot represents one village

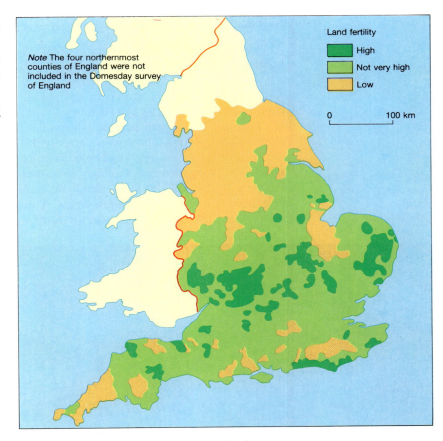

*Note* The four northernmost counties of England were not included in the Domesday survey of England

Land fertility
- High
- Not very high
- Low

0        100 km

Using the map and your atlases, list the following areas under **A** or **B**: the Weald; the Thames valley; eastern Norfolk; the Fens; the New Forest; the Sussex coast; the Pennines; the Cotswolds. Give reasons for the areas you have included under **B**.

*Above:* A map of land fertility in Norman England based on the information in *Domesday Book*.

# 9 Medieval fields

Take a piece of ridged cardboard – the sort often used as packing material. Move it around under a light. There will be no shadows if the light comes from above. If the light comes from an angle, one side of each ridge will be in the shadow of the other. The picture below shows the same effect. From which direction is the sunlight coming? Why are there so many shadows running in straight lines?

The picture shows medieval fields. Each field is made up of many straight ridges and furrows. These strips are grouped into blocks or **furlongs**. In each furlong the strips run the same way. The view in the picture is mostly of one large field made up of several furlongs. The hedges in the picture were planted at a later date – try to ignore these when looking for the different furlongs. All these patterns show up much more easily on a sunny day when there are shadows than on a cloudy one.

## Padbury: a medieval village

The strips and furlongs shown in the photograph belong to the village of Padbury, Buckinghamshire. They were part of a large field called the Hedge Field. The area covered by the picture is shown on the medieval map of Padbury. Most of medieval Padbury consisted of three fields – the Hedge Field, East Field, and West Field. They were **common fields**. This means that instead of each peasant farmer having his own separate piece of land, he shared the fields with other farmers. Each farmer would have several strips in each of the three fields. This might seem a complicated way of dividing up land, but it made sense. Everybody had a share of both the fertile and poorer land. The common fields were also open – that is, there were no fences or hedges between the strips or furlongs. Various track-ways like the 'Whadden Way' were used by villagers every day to go from the village to outlying parts of the fields.

Medieval people knew how important it was to change the crops grown in each field from year to year. When the same crop is grown every year, the soil gradually becomes infertile. Growing a different crop each year helps to keep the soil in good condition. They also knew the importance of leaving soil **fallow** for a year – that is, bare, without any crop at all. The Padbury farmers kept the soil fertile by using a system of **rotation**. In one year they would grow wheat in the Hedge Field and barley in the East Field. The West Field would be fallow. The following year the West Field might have wheat, the Hedge Field barley, and the East Field fallow.

*Far right:* The medieval field system around Padbury.

*Below:* A landscape of medieval open fields at Padbury, Buckinghamshire.

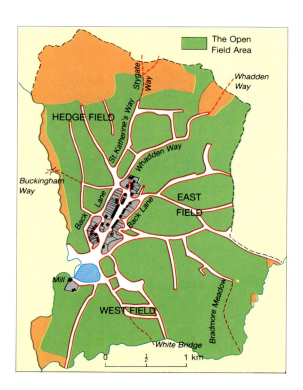

## The farmer's year

Throughout the farmer's year the weather determined what work could be done. The farmer's success or failure and the very life of his family, also depended on the weather. If the spring was very cold, the seeds in the ground would be slow to start growing, and the plants might not have time to grow fully before the autumn. If the summer was cold and wet the crop would not ripen properly. In either case there was less grain available for making flour and bread, and the family would go hungry.

In the diagram the farmer is ploughing his field in the autumn. Why do you think *four* oxen were needed to pull the plough? What does this tell you about the plough – and about the soil? You can see from the diagram how ploughing was done, and how each strip came to have its 'ridge and furrow' shape.

## How typical was Padbury?

In the midland and eastern counties of England, a lot of villages were like Padbury. Almost all their land lay in open, common fields. Elsewhere, common fields were not always so wide-spread. In hilly areas with poor soil, common fields were often very small and most of the land was pasture. Villagers depended more on grazing animals and less on crops for their livelihoods.

In history it is often very unsafe to generalize about something from just one example. Padbury is typical of medieval villages in many ways, but we would be wrong to expect all villages to have been just like Padbury. Historians look at the ways in which places differed, as well as the ways in which they were alike. □

*Above:* Areas of England and Wales which had many common fields are shown shaded.

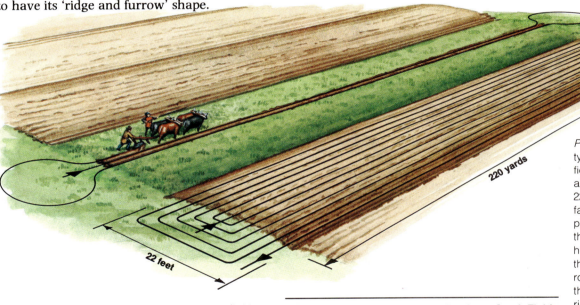

*Ploughing a Strip:* A typical strip in the open fields might have been about 22 feet wide and 220 yards long. The farmer would start to plough his strip just to the left of centre. When he reached the end of the row he would turn round and come back the other way, just to the right of the first line. He carried on in this way, working outwards to the edge of the strip until it was all ploughed.

The earth was always thrown to the right by the plough, and the centre of the strip became built upwards into a 'ridge' while the outside formed a 'furrow'. This helped to keep the land well drained.

1 Suppose a medieval village has three fields – North Field, East Field, and South Field. A peasant farmer has strips in each of the three fields. He grows wheat and barley. Copy and complete the calendar on the right to show how he uses each of his fields during a three-year period. Include the various tasks he carries out in each field. You will need to read the text again. You will also need to know that: wheat is autumn sown; barley is spring sown; barley follows wheat in each field; wheat follows fallow; livestock graze the stubble after harvesting. Use a system of colour shading to make the diagram more effective.

2 Write a paragraph explaining why the surface of medieval fields was not flat.

3 'In hilly areas with poor soil there were fewer common fields'. Study the map in the right hand column and compare it with the map on page 19 and with a relief map in your atlases. Do you think the statement is true?

| YEAR 1 | Hedge Field | East Field | South Field |
|---|---|---|---|
| Spring | Fallow | Sowing barley | |
| Summer | | Harvesting barley | Harvesting wheat |
| Autumn | Ploughing | Grazing stubble | Grazing stubble |
| | Sowing wheat | | |
| | | Fallow | Ploughing |
| YEAR 2 | Hedge Field | East Field | South Field |

# 10 Going to market

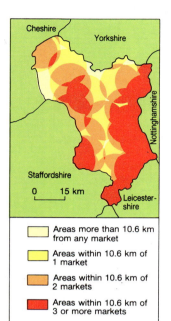

*Above:* Henry de Bracton, a medieval lawyer, worked out that a reasonable day's journey to market was no more than 7 miles (10.6 km). The trader would spend a third of the day getting there, a third in buying and selling, and a third in going home. How well does his idea work in Derbyshire?

Medieval markets were busy, bustling, noisy places. The market was held in a large open space or 'square' in the middle of the town or village. Sometimes the market square really was square in shape. Elsewhere it was just a space formed where the main street widened out. Look at the aerial view of Chipping Campden, Gloucestershire. The name 'chipping' itself means 'market'. Find where the main street widens out to form the market square. Why do you think there is not as much open space there now? What has happened to it?

Going to market was a regular part of village life. Tradesmen and farmers needed somewhere to sell their products and food. At that time travelling was very slow and most people walked. So markets had to be near where people lived. A medieval lawyer called Henry de Bracton even worked out that no one should live more than seven miles from a market. He thought that this was the furthest that people could reasonably walk to market in a day. Remember that they had a lot of things to carry, and they had to walk home afterwards too. Even if the farmer had a horse and cart he did not travel much faster. How often do you walk 14 miles a day?

## Where were the markets?

All towns and larger villages had markets. Bakers, cobblers, tailors, and potters could all be found there, besides many other traders. Look at the list. How many of these traders would you find at a market today? People also came to sell their oxen, sheep, pigs, and hens, and geese. On market day every bit of spare space would have been taken up by sellers shouting their wares and arguing their prices with buyers. The market was one of the main events of the week.

Not every place could set up a market. A royal charter, or letter of authority from the king, was needed. Read the charter below, granted by Henry I in 1105 to the abbey of Tavistock, Devon. It allowed the monks to hold a market in the town of Tavistock. What do you think the last few words mean?

*Right:* Chipping Campden, an old market town in Gloucestershire. The market place was in the broadest part of the main street, now occupied by an island of buildings.

Henry, King of England, to the barons of Devon and Cornwall greetings Know that I have granted to the abbey of St. Mary of Tavistock and to the monks a market in Tavistock every week on Friday. And I grant to the merchants that they may buy and sell whatever they please there and no one is to do them wrong

Market centres competed with each other for trade just as supermarkets and department stores do today. At Steeple Ashton in Wiltshire a new Wednesday market was started in 1266.

It was too successful for the owner of the old market at nearby Market Lavington. He complained that he had lost £40 in two years because of the new market. This would be worth £50,000 today.

Many towns still have a market cross. This was put up to show traders and customers that they would be safe from attacks by robbers and outlaws while they carried out their business. Some market centres had market halls. The one from Titchfield, Hampshire, has been taken apart and put together again at an open-air museum. From the upper room the market officers would watch to see that there was fair trading. The space below the upper room was for very poor people who could not afford their own stalls.

## A medieval map of England

An old map known as the Gough map shows several medieval market towns and the roads joining them. Even if you live in the area covered by the extract, your own town might not be shown. This is because many of today's towns and cities were very small places in the Middle Ages. Norwich, Bristol, and York were some of the main cities of medieval England. □

*Above:* The market hall at Ledbury, Hereford and Worcestershire.

*Below:* An extract from a medieval map of England. London is in the middle, north is on the left. With the help of a modern atlas try to find Reading, Dover, and Colchester.

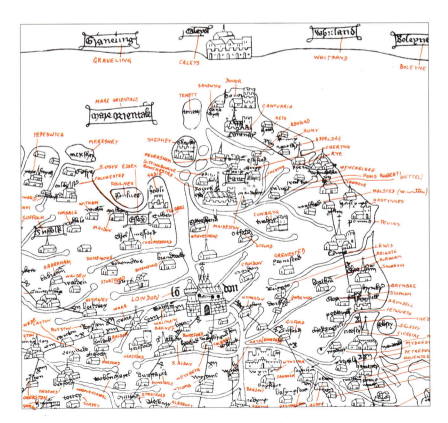

1 List the features in the landscape by which you might recognize an old market town. Now use your list to draw a picture of medieval market square on market day. Use the pictures on these pages to help you.

2 Study the map on page 22. It shows how far apart places in Derbyshire were from their nearest market. Was Bracton right in what he thought?

3 Why do you think the poorer traders might welcome the use of the lower space in market halls?

4 Several places have been mentioned in this section, all in different counties. Can you remember them all? List them in a table like the one below:

| County | Example of market town or village |
|---|---|
| Gloucestershire | Chipping Campden |
| | |

If you know of other old market towns, add them too.

5 Explain why market towns were so important to medieval people.

# 11 A castle town

The photograph opposite shows a place called Milton Keynes. It is a new English city which has been built in the middle of the Bedfordshire countryside. When it is finished it will have over 300,000 people. It is so big that it has absorbed several towns and villages nearby. This city is taking over 25 years to complete. It was being planned for many years even before building started.

We would be wrong to think that building new towns is a modern idea. Seven hundred years ago King Edward I built a lot of new towns. A number of them are in North Wales. In 1283 he had just finished his conquest of Wales. He decided that the best way to hold on to his power in the country was to build a series of towns. Each town would attract English settlers who would encourage trade and peace with the native Welsh. But the towns would also have strong castles and many soldiers. In the event of a rebellion, troops could then be moved quickly into the surrounding countryside to deal with the trouble.

*Far right:* Milton Keynes, a new town built very recently.

*Below:* Caernarfon, Wales, planned by King Edward I in the 13th century.

## Caernarfon: a castle town

Caernarfon was one of these castle towns, or **bastides** as they are sometimes called. There was already a Norman castle at Caernarfon but Edward wanted something much bigger. Building Caernarfon was a huge task for which stonemasons, smiths, and carpenters had to be brought from England. Much of the town was built by the 1290s, but the castle itself was not finished until 1327. It has 13 towers, and was built so that any one tower could be held even if the rest of the castle had been captured. The castle was protected by the sea and river on the south and west sides and by a moat on the northern and eastern sides.

North of the castle, Edward laid out a new town as carefully as any modern town planner. His town had long straight streets which crossed each other at right angles. The land facing on to these streets was divided up into equally sized plots, each 24 m by 18 m. Each plot was rented or sold to an English settler. There were about 70 of these plots altogether. Each plot was called a **burgage**, and its occupier was a **burgess**. Most of Caernarfon's burgesses would have been shop owners or tradesmen who lived above their businesses. The whole town was enclosed by a strong wall with two main gates.

# The changing townscape

The word **townscape** refers to the landscape of a town – the appearance and use of the various buildings, and the layout of the streets and open spaces. Look at the plan of Caernarfon made in 1610. This shows the townscape 300 years after the town was built. Find on it the castle, the town wall, and the medieval town of Edward I. What had happened to the town since Edward I's time? Suggest some reasons why it had spread outside the medieval walls. Why do you think the walls were not as important to Caernarfon in 1610 as they had been in the thirteenth century?

Look at the modern town plan. Caernarfon is now much bigger than it was in earlier times. It spreads up on to the surrounding hillsides beyond the edge of the map. The castle is still there and most of the wall survives. How many of the old street names can you still find? John Speed wrote many of the names in English, but nowadays they are usually written in Welsh. Notice how you can pick out where the medieval town was from its regular street pattern. The pattern has survived into the modern townscape. But there is hardly anything left of Edward I's burgage plots – they were all divided into smaller plots and sold off for new buildings long ago. However the modern market hall still occupies a plot of this size – perhaps this is an old burgage plot which has remained unchanged until the present day.

Today the old streets and walls of Caernarfon see many visitors. The links with Welsh history and royalty ensure that it remains an important tourist attraction. Princes of Wales, including the present one, are still invested at Caernarfon. □

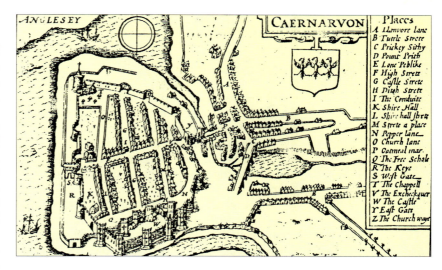

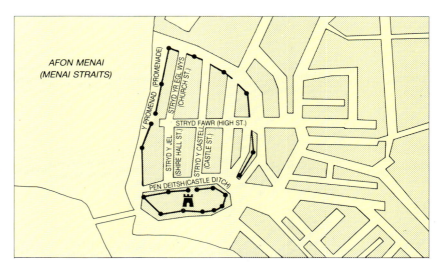

*Above:* John Speed's map of Caernarfon 1610 (top) and Caernarfon today (bottom).

1 Read again about 'fossil landscapes' (page 8). Would you agree that Caernarfon is also a fossil landscape? Give your reasons.

2 Make a tracing outlining the area covered by present-day Caernarfon. Use colours to shade in: the area covered by Edward I's medieval town; the area built up between Edward's time and 1610; the area built up since 1610.

Add the castle, quayside, market square, and any other detail you like. Call your drawing 'How Caernarfon's townscape has changed over the centuries'.

3 What sorts of things would an English stonemason working at Caernarfon around 1295 be able to tell his friends at home about?

4 Ask your geography teacher to tell you more about Milton Keynes and other new towns being built today. Are there any similarities with the reasons for building Caernarfon?

## Edward I's other castle towns

Edward I's other bastides in North Wales are Denbigh, Rhuddlan, Flint, Conwy, Harlech, Cricieth, and Beaumaris. They were all built as part of a master plan, to surround the Welsh strongholds in the mountains with castles. They were mostly on or close to the coast. In this way they could be kept supplied by sea during a siege. The King's towns were very well planned and they have all survived as towns to the present day.

# 12 Two medieval houses

Have you been into the loft of a house? A lot of people use their lofts for storing suitcases, trunks, old junk, and odds-and-ends. If you shine a torch around the inside of the roof you can see all the beams and rafters. How do they all fit together? Different kinds of joints are used.

Look at the diagram below of a medieval open hall. Unless you live in a very old house, it is unlikely that the timbers in your loft will look the same as this. This sort of roof was common in medieval houses. Notice how important the timbers called **crown posts** were – try to imagine what might happen if you took them away.

A medieval open hall. Notice the crown post (**A**), tie beam (**B**), collar (**C**), crown plate (**D**) and rafter (**E**).

## A lord's house

The hall in the picture below is part of the house of a fairly wealthy person. Houses like this were built at about the time of the Black Death. The main room was called an 'open hall' because there was no upstairs and no ceiling. From the mud floor you could look straight up into the roof.

Houses had very little furniture at this time. The main item of furniture was often the 'high table', where the lord of the house took his meals. Even the wealthiest homes had only the minimum of furnishings with a few woven tapestries on the walls.

People would have spent their evenings keeping warm and dry around the open hearth in the middle of the floor. From here the smoke curled upwards and escaped through gaps in the roof, which was thatched. The loftier the roof was, the less danger there was from the thatch catching fire. The walls were made of timber frames. The spaces between the posts were filled in with 'wattle-and-daub', a sort of basketwork covered with dried mud. Some spaces were not covered over but left for windows. Tapestries and shutters would be pulled across them in wet weather.

We would find this house draughty, smoky, and very cold in winter. But to most medieval people it would have seemed very comfortable. Besides the great hall there were other, smaller, rooms – such as a pantry, kitchen, and chambers (private rooms). In the picture you can see the doors leading to these rooms. Houses like these belonged to knights, merchants, and wealthy people. These were the only people well-off enough to build houses with huge open halls and extra separate rooms.

## A peasant's house

Ordinary people had much simpler houses. At the village of Wharram Percy in North Yorkshire, archaeologists found the remains of several medieval peasant houses. From these remains, they have made up a picture of one of them. Like the medieval hall, it was made of timber, wattle, and thatch. It was quite narrow and long. At one end the family cooked, ate, slept, made their clothes, and repaired their

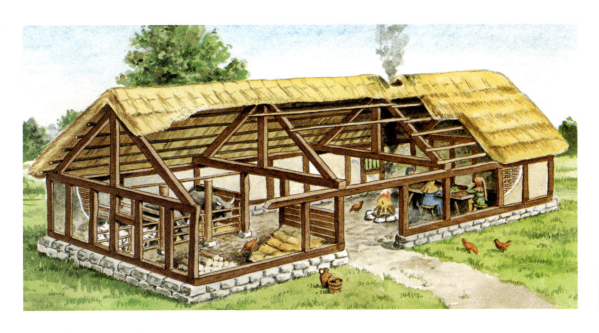

*Left:* An artist's impression of one of the Wharram Percy houses.

tools. The other or 'lower' end of the house was used to shelter oxen and sheep. Fuel and grain would also be stored there. During the day the hens and geese would strut all round the house looking for scraps of food on the mud floor. The house would probably have been built by the family who lived in it, with help from friends or neighbours.

We might think that living in this house was not much different from living in a barn or cowshed. But less than 100 years ago in some parts of Scotland and Ireland, people still slept in the same room as their cattle.

## Some other medieval houses

There were other sorts of medieval houses besides the ones described. In Devon, Cornwall, Wales, and Scotland they were usually built of stone instead of wood. Some of them looked rather like the 'crofters' cottages you can sometimes find in Scotland.

In the cities of Africa, South America, and Asia, millions of people today live in very poor, ramshackle houses. They build them from cardboard boxes, plastic sheets, tyres, oil drums, and any other cast-off materials they can find. Perhaps beggars and down-and-out people in medieval cities lived in much the same way. They would have used straw, mud, and odd pieces of wood to build tiny hovels. Inside they would huddle for shelter from the rain and wind. We really know very little about what their houses looked like, because none has survived. □

*Left:* The houses of very poor people in a South American city today. In the Middle Ages the houses of the poorest people would have been just as flimsy.

1 The diagram shows a complicated wooden joint. It was used in medieval houses where the roof and wall posts meet. Imagine that the carpenter hasn't shaped the bottom post yet (marked X). It has to fit into the other pieces. Can you redraw this bottom post to show how he might have shaped it?

2 Make a list of the similarities and differences between the two types of medieval houses shown here. Use these headings: number of rooms; size of main room; sharing rooms with cattle; quality of woodwork; building materials; heating.

3 Now do the same for the Wimbish house and your own home. Use the same headings. Add more headings if you need them.

4 Why do you think so few medieval houses have survived to the present?

5 Some people think that medieval house-building was rough and primitive. From what you have seen in the pictures and diagrams, would you agree?

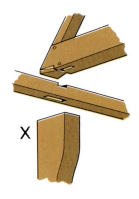

*Above:* Tie beam lap dovetail assembly.

# 13 A deer park

It had been a busy week for the park keeper. In the space of a few days he had cut several cartloads of branches and twigs to plug the gaps in the fence. As winter was coming on, he had cut some loads of young tree shoots for the park animals to graze on. He had also fenced off a portion of the park to rent to local farmers for grazing their cattle. Finally he had cut and stacked a load of turf to keep the park lodge in fuel over the winter.

What sort of park do you think this was? It wasn't a town park where we might walk the dog or see friends; nor, despite the mention of animals, was it a game or safari park. This park keeper was in charge of a 'deer park'. Most medieval lords had their deer parks. These were fenced-off areas where deer could be bred and hunted. Deer and wild game always belonged to lords, who liked nothing better than to go hunting. Keeping deer in parks protected the animals against being hunted by poachers. Medieval lords employed park keepers to look after their parks carefully, to keep out poachers, and to make sure that there were always enough deer for them to hunt.

Leagram was a medieval deer park in Bowland Forest, Lancashire. The area shaded green was the better quality grassland. Much of the rest of the part was marshy land called *carr* or *moss*.

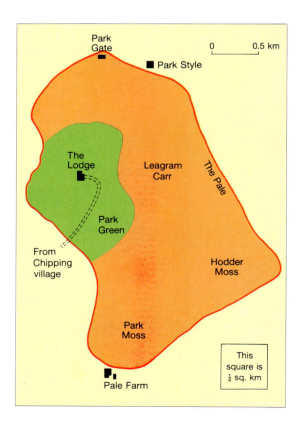

## Leagram Park

The park shown in the map on the left was at Leagram, near Chipping, in Lancashire. It was made round about the year 1340 for the Duke of Lancaster. The park wall or fence was called a 'pale' because it was made of long poles or 'palings' of split oaks. These were placed close together in the ground and stood several feet high on top of an earthen bank. Inside the bank was a ditch 8 ft wide and about 4 ft deep. Rows of thorns were planted on both sides of the bank to keep out poachers.

Even today you can still see where the pale was. On the map, notice the farms called Park Gate, Park Style, and Pale Farm. These all follow the line of the pale, which you can probably pick out quite easily. They show how the names of farms can sometimes tell us something about an area's history. Parts of the old bank are still in use today to mark field boundaries.

Do you know of any areas near where you live that were once deer parks? How much is left of them now?

## Bowland Forest

Leagram was one of two deer parks in the Forest of Bowland. In the fourteenth century, Bowland would have been a wild, bleak area of dense woods, rushing streams, barren open moors, and mountainous crags. This made it an ideal hunting area. The lords of Bowland Forest jealously guarded their hunting rights; they had very severe forest laws for people caught poaching. You might have had your hands cut off for being found in any of the situations described below.

---

**Poaching terms**

**Bloody hand** Standing over a dead deer with your hands covered in blood

**Dog-dray** Using hounds to chase a wounded deer

**Stable-stand** Having a bow drawn, ready to shoot an arrow

**Back-bear** Carrying away a dead deer over your shoulder

---

*Above:* A Bowland Forest landscape today. People found poaching here by foresters in medieval times were severely punished. Some were fined, some even had their hands cut off.

The setting up of new farms or villages in the forest was also discouraged in order to keep people away.

As time went on, however, the lords of Bowland came to be more concerned with how much money they could earn from their forests. Although they still applied the forest laws, they became mostly interested in how much they could fine people for killing the deer. Special forest courts called 'woodmotes' were held. At these courts, people who had been found poaching deer were summoned and fined. There were also fines for cutting down trees and using the timber for building. The fines were not really intended to stop people from taking deer and wood. They were really meant as payment for what had been taken from the forest.

## Disafforestation

One lord of Bowland in about 1250 was even more enterprising. He turned over large areas of Bowland Forest to 'vaccaries' (cattle ranches). In this way Bowland gradually became less of a forest and more of a farming area. As it did so, the old forest laws gradually fell into disuse. This is what **disafforestation** means – doing away with the forest laws.

*Left:* A hunting party returning home.

29

Upon the Holy Rood even there were hunters in the said forest who put a leash of greyhounds at the deer in a place called the Holly Field; which dogs came running at a hind near Hugh Hodgekinson's house in the said forest.

We present Christopher Coote for killing one buck in Whitendale in the said forest about the Nativity of Our Lady with his greyhounds.

John Bleasdale for taking a sapling without payment to the repair of his own house, fine 12d

Thomas Bradley of Thornley for felling one great alder within the said forest, fine 6d

William Isherwood for cropping of the saplings and felling of yarding at inconvenient times of the year.

There are many other farming areas in Britain which were once forests. You may know the New Forest, where some forest regulations still apply. Everybody has heard of Sherwood Forest of the Robin Hood legend. But even at the time of the legend, it was as much a farming area as a forested one. □

1 How big was Leagram Park? This exercise will teach you how to measure area.
  a) On a piece of tracing paper draw the outline of the park.
  b) Cover the tracing paper with a grid of squares each 0.25 sq km. A square of the right size is already drawn for you.
  c) Write a '1' inside each square lying *completely inside* the park boundary. Write a 'O' inside each square lying *completely outside* the park boundary. Write a '1' inside a square if *more* than half of it lies inside the park boundary. Write a 'O' inside a square if *less* than half of it lies inside the park boundary. Now count up the number of squares with '1'.
  d) Remember that each square with '1' is 0.25 sq km
  e) Now work out total area = number of '1' squares × 0.25 sq km
     = _____ sq km
  f) Compare your result with others from your class. Find the average result. This will be quite an accurate answer.

2 Explain why Bowland was: a) made into a forest; b) later disafforested.

3 The term 'forest' comes from a word meaning 'outside the law.' In what ways were forests outside the ordinary law?

4 'Medieval forests were wild, unmanaged places.' After reading these pages, would you agree?

# Some terms used in this book

Terms included in the glossary appear in bold where they first appear in the text.

**Aerial photograph** A photograph of the landscape taken from a low-flying aeroplane. Some are *vertical* (taken straight from above), others are *oblique* (taken from an angle).

**Ancient monument** A structure surviving from prehistoric times. Ancient monuments include barrows, stone circles, hill forts, and other *earthworks*.

**Archaeology** The study of the past from the remains left by earlier peoples. Archaeologists are especially concerned with prehistoric times, before there were written records.

**Barrow** A prehistoric burial mound. Entire families might be buried in a single barrow.

**Bastide** A medieval fortress town. It was built to subdue and secure the region around it.

**Burgage** A plot of land in a medieval town. It would often be occupied by the house and business premises of an important citizen. The occupier of a burgage was a **burgess**.

**Burgess** The holder of a burgage. He was usually an important citizen, businessman, trader, etc.

**Common field** A field shared and worked by the whole village, not just by one farmer. Common fields were *open* (without hedges) and were worked in **rotation** with other fields.

**Crown Post** A vertical post found in the roof of a medieval house.

**Disafforestation** The abolition of forest laws in an area. This usually encouraged more people to settle and live in the area, creating new farms, hamlets, and villages.

**Earthwork** A bank made of earth, indicating the site of an earlier building or fortification. Earthworks are often the only evidence in the landscape of important prehistoric buildings or structures.

**Excavation** Digging up a site to find remains from the past. Successful excavation needs to be planned and carried out very carefully.

**Fallow** Land left bare of crops, so that it can recover its fertility.

**Furlong** A block of strips in a common field, 220 yds long. A furlong would have its own name, and a common field might contain several furlongs. The name was also used as a measurement of length, i.e. 220 yds or one-eighth of a mile.

**Hill-fort** A hilltop fortification of Iron Age times. Many of them had several sets of **ramparts** and complicated defences and gates. Archaeologists describe such hill-forts as 'multivallate'.

*Left:* Barbury Castle, an Iron Age Hill-fort in Wiltshire.

**Prehistoric** Very early times, from which few written records have survived. In Britain all ages before the coming of the Romans are called prehistoric.

**Radiocarbon dating** A method of dating which is based on the rate of radioactive decay in substances. Dates so identified are thought to be accurate up to $\pm$ five per cent of the age calculated.

**Rampart** A defensive wall or earthwork in fortifications.

**Rotation** Growing a crop in different fields each year. In this way each field has a different crop every year. This helps to maintain the land's fertility. Rotation usually includes a **fallow** year.

**Townscape** The landscape of a town. Buildings, streets, and open spaces are all part of the townscape.

**Tundra** Very cold regions with frozen mosses and swamps, and very few trees. Most of Britain was tundra in early prehistoric times.

# Index

Illustration references are shown in heavy type

**Acknowledgements**
The publishers would like to thank the following for permission to produce photographs:

AA Photolibrary, p 29; Aerofilms, pp 2–3, 13, 31; Biofotos, p 8 (top); Janet and Colin Bord, pp 6, 15; British Library, p 29; British Tourist Authority, pp 4 (top), 23; Committee for Aerial Photography, University of Cambridge, pp 7 (top), 10, 11, 20, 22; G. Gerster, p 31; Alastair Gray, p 27; Susan Griggs, pp 12, 17 (both); English Heritage, p 4 (bottom); Mike Holford, p 16; National Monuments Record, p 8 (bottom); John Porter, p 9, p 28/29; Public Record Office, p 18 (right) Charlotte Ward-Perkins, p 18 (left); West Air Photography p 24 (both).

Illustrations by Carol Kemp and Melvyn Wright.

Cover illustration: Knowlton Rings, Dorset (G. Gerster).

**Oxford University Press, Walton St, Oxford OX2 6DP**

Oxford  New York  Toronto
Delhi  Bombay  Calcutta  Madras  Karachi
Petaling Jaya  Singapore  Hong Kong  Tokyo
Nairobi  Dar es Salaam  Cape Town
Melbourne  Auckland

*and associated companies in*
Berlin  Ibadan
*Oxford* is a trademark of Oxford University Press

© **Oxford University Press 1988**

ISBN 0 19 913315 8 (limp, non-net)
ISBN 0 19 913348 4 (cased, net)

Typesetting by MS Filmsetting Ltd, Frome, Somerset
Printed in Hong Kong